BRAIN GAMES™

Dare to Doodle

Publications International, Ltd.

Art credits:
Art Explosion, Dover Publications, iStockphoto, Jupiterimages, Shutterstock

Illustrators: Jeff Moores and Erin Burke

Jeff Moores is an illustrator whose work appears in periodicals and advertisements
and as licensed characters on clothing. Visit his Web sites (jeffmoores.com and findharri.com)
to see more of his work.

Louis Weber, CEO
Publications International, Ltd.
7373 North Cicero Avenue
Lincolnwood, Illinois 60712

ISBN-13: 978-1-4508-3437-7
ISBN-10: 1-4508-3437-X

Manufactured in China.

8 7 6 5 4 3 2 1

Dare to Doodle

Who says doodling is just for kids? Whether you're young in years or young at heart, pick up a pen and simply let your mind wander —you may be surprised at the results!

Can't think of anything to draw? *Dare to Doodle* has you covered! Flip open this book, and inside you'll find tons of fun and easy drawing suggestions and prompts that will tap your creative side and give the right side of your brain a good workout.

Seriously, this isn't fine art, and there's no way to screw this up —just relax, do a little doodlin', and have fun!

Finish the cover of this horror novel.
Don't forget to add a bone-chilling title!

Design the vacation stickers on this suitcase. Au revoir!

Color in the pattern to make new designs. Shouldn't bee too hard, right?

Score! Decorate the superfan's shirt, hat, and foam finger with his favorite team's logo.

Who's a *widdle pwecious* kitty? Dress these cats in outfits,
and add another feline into the mix.

Don't get carried away by these waves.

Take this repeating pattern and go with the flow!

I'M RICH!

Design this paper and coin currency.
Now go buy yourself something nice.

Make a neighborhood map!

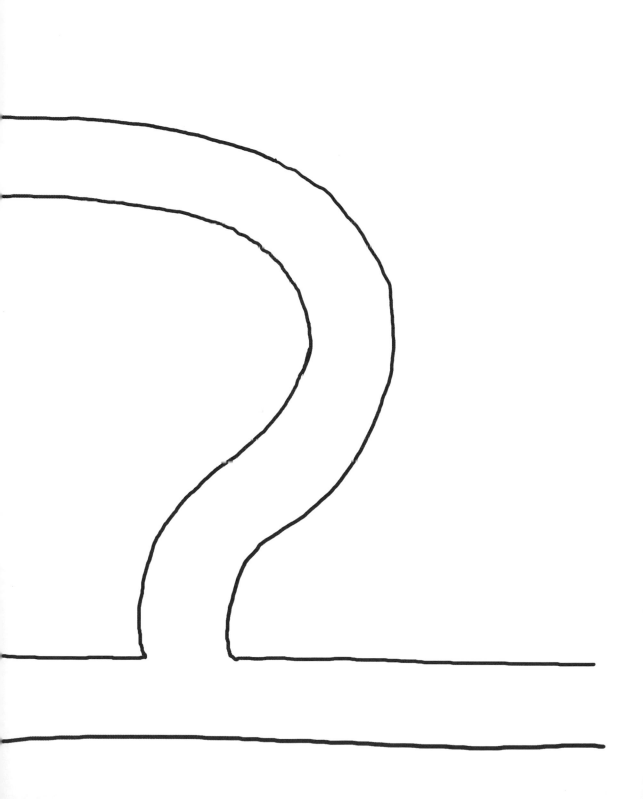

Hmm. Since you're already snooping in the medicine cabinet, why don't you go ahead and draw what's in there?

This is quite the party! Finish drawing the people and decor.

Sweet! They have that CD you've been looking for!

What's inside this snow globe? Shake it up a bit!

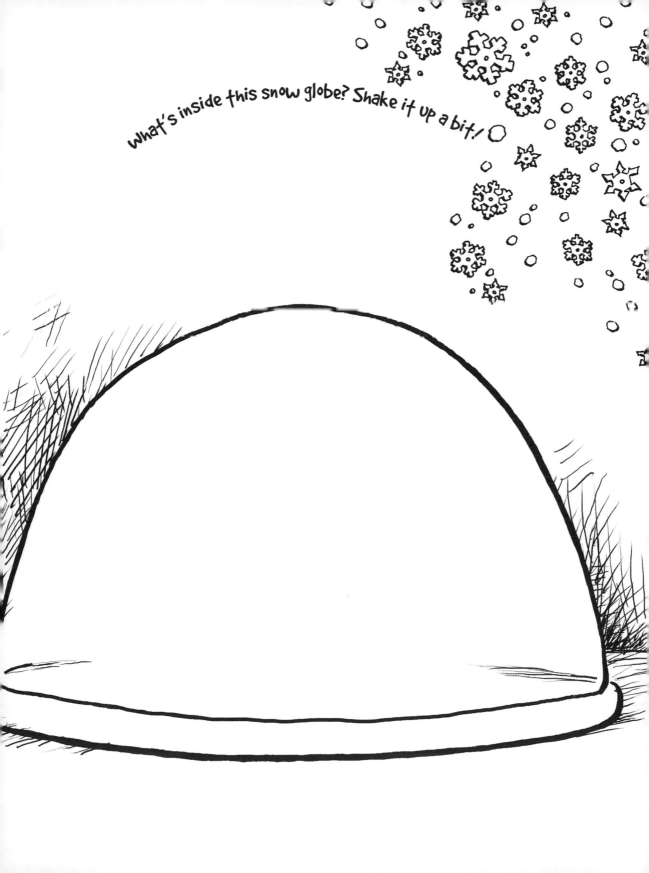

Add hair, features, and whatever else you'd like
to these lovely lady mannequins.

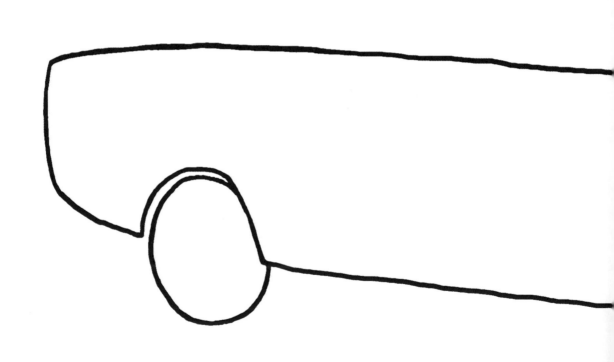

What a sweet ride! Finish drawing and decorating this custom vintage car.

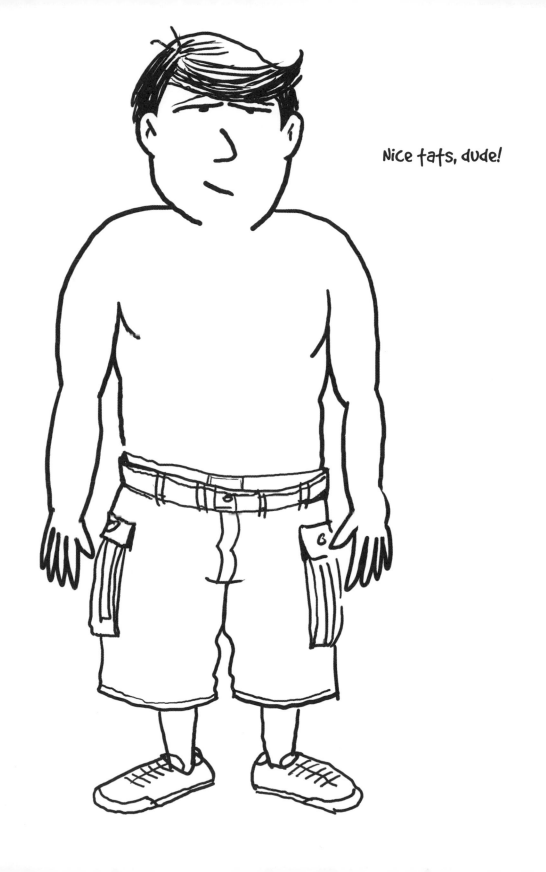

Nice tats, dude!

Finish drawing the layout of your future home.

WELCOME

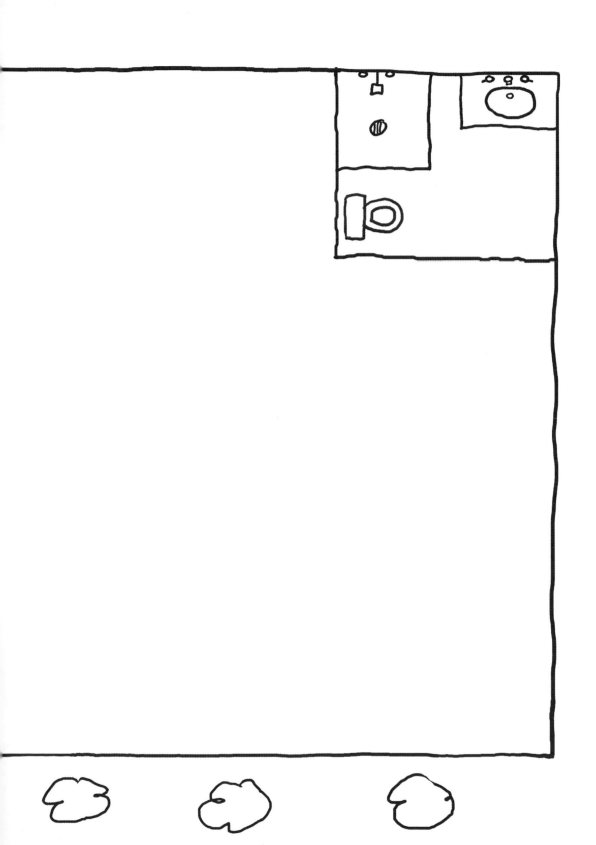

Take this repeating pattern and run with it!

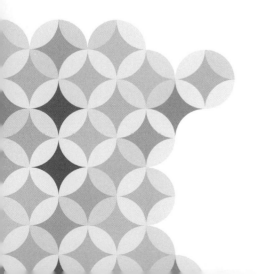

ooh-la-la! Design the labels on these fancy perfume bottles.

finish these numerals, and try to keep up the fancy font.

1 2 3

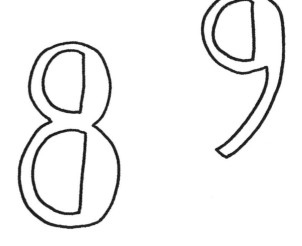

Uh-oh, looks like trouble's afoot! Draw the last panel of this comic strip.

Aren't you sweet?
Decorate these candy hearts,
or add sweet messages!

Finish illustrating this romance novel's cover.
Don't forget to add a breathtaking title!

Portrait time! What did you look like when you were ten years old?
Include props and surroundings.

Design the jewelry in this display case.

GOALPOST GOALPOST GOALPOST GOALPOST

GOALPOST GOALPOST GOALPOST GOALPOST

GOAL POST GOAL POST GOALPOST

GOALPOST GOALPOST

See if you can finish this picture incorporating words into the drawing!

Don't strike out—design your bowling league's shirt!

Looks like the safari hunter met his match. What did he find?

Add bits and pieces to this outrageous tutti-frutti hat!

we started this crazy doodle—keep it going!

Design these collectible postage stamps.

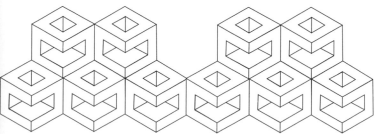

Continue drawing this repeating pattern. Fill in the shading to make it cooler!

Finish drawing yonder castle! Be sure to add scenery and other details.

Hope you're not afraid of heights!
Decorate these hot air balloons and add scenery.

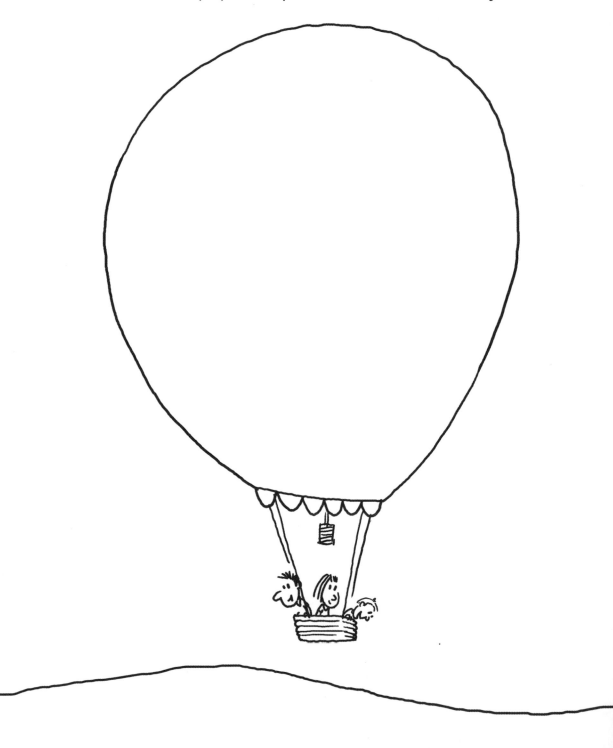

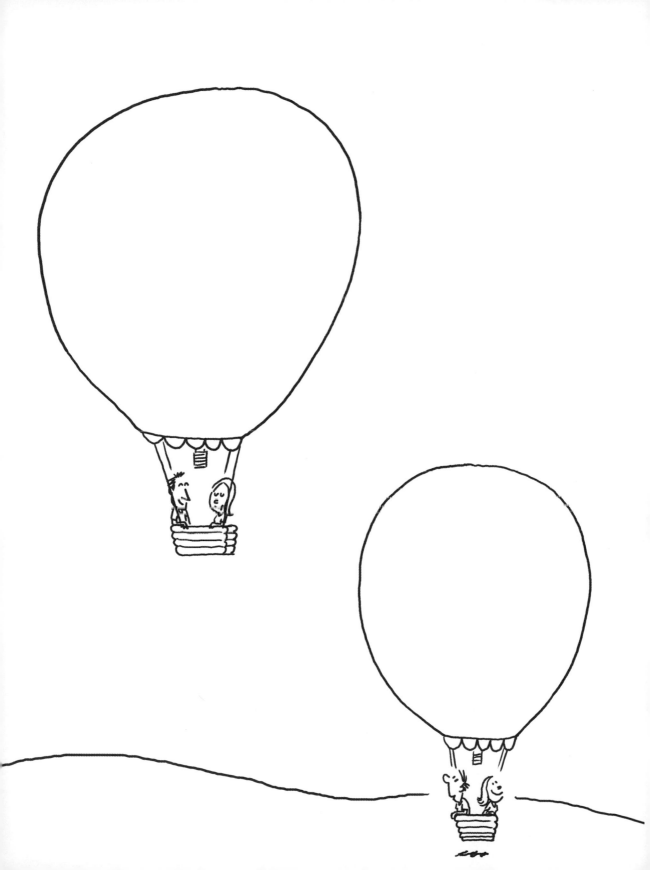

congratulations!
What awards did you win?

what's this catnapping kitty dreaming about?

It's hip to be square! fill in the squares to create new patterns.

Want a snack? Draw what's inside!

Hey, looking is free, right?
What's in the department store display window?

Get these two ready for work!

You've just published a cookbook! Draw the rest of the cover illustration, and don't forget to give it a mouthwatering title!

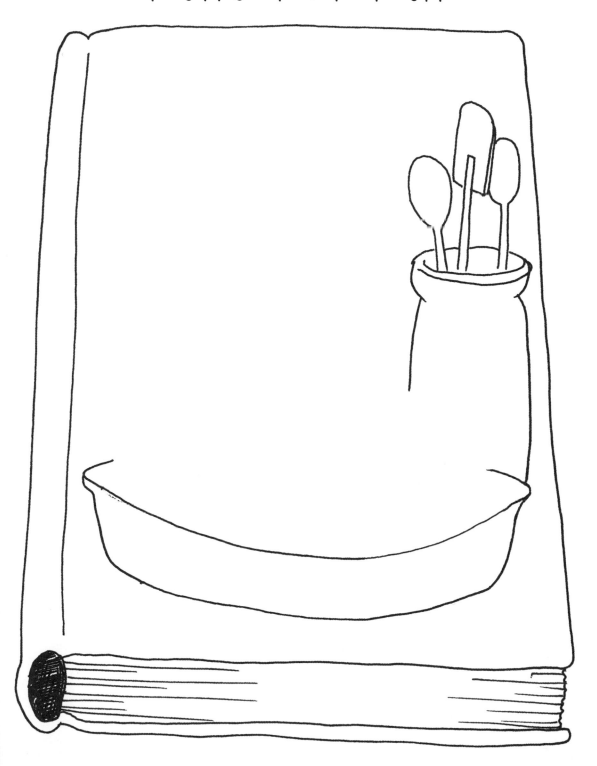

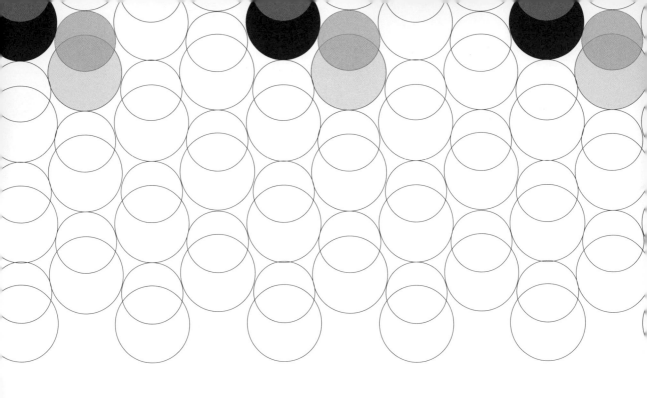

Take this repeating pattern and roll with it!

Strap on your scuba gear! What do you sea?

We drew this cup o' joe using related words. Come up with one of your own!

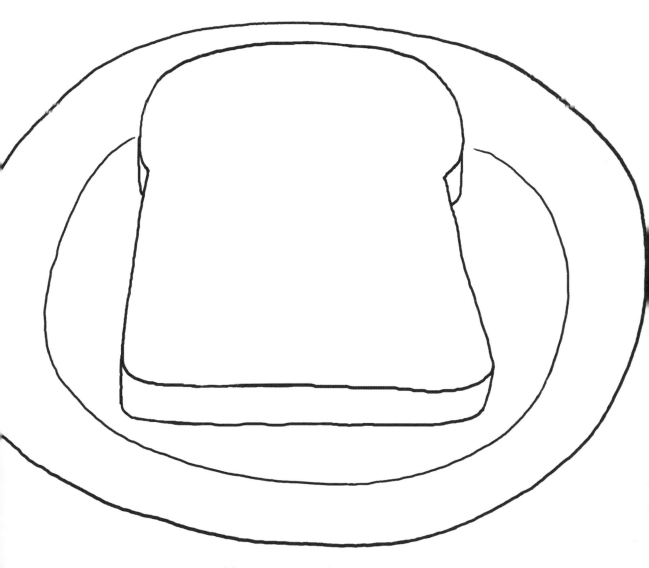

Mm-mmm! That looks like a mighty fine sandwich. What's on it?

Dig in, and finish drawing this scene!

what's on this computer screensaver?

You see what we were going for. Now it's your turn to draw the repeating pattern!

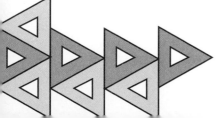

Finish drawing the spider web, and add more spider snacks.

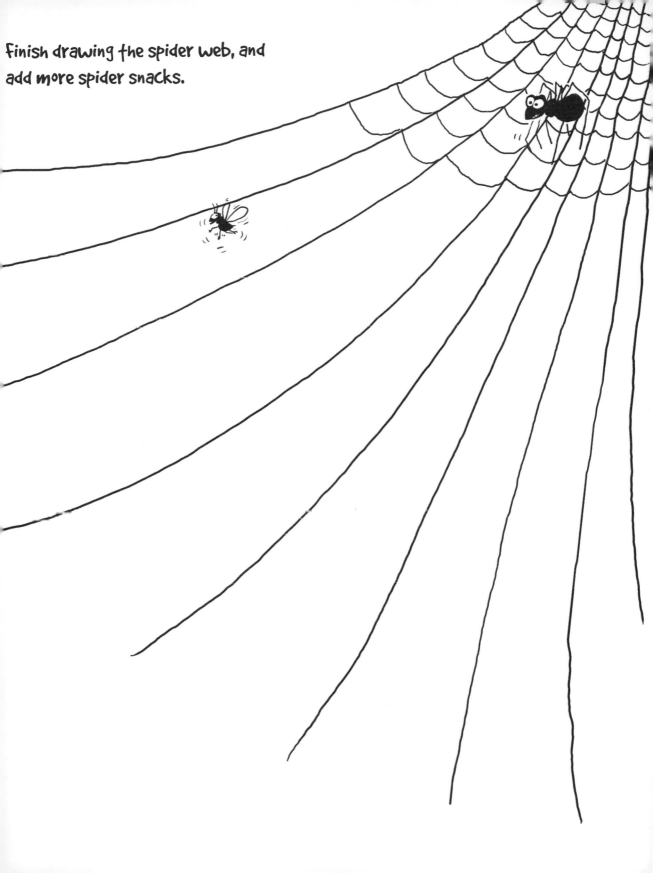

Go team! Finish drawing the helmet and pennant.

Draw the mirror image of this pattern.

Finish the alphabet, and try to keep up the fractured font!

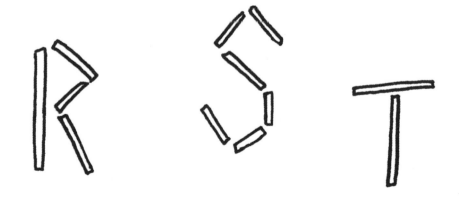

What three things would you bring to a desert island? Draw them here!

oh man, these cakes look *so good*.
finish drawing and decorating them!

How does your garden grow?

Decorate these coffee mugs, just waiting to be filled with hot brew...

Color in the pattern to make new designs.

Decorate these cool kicks.

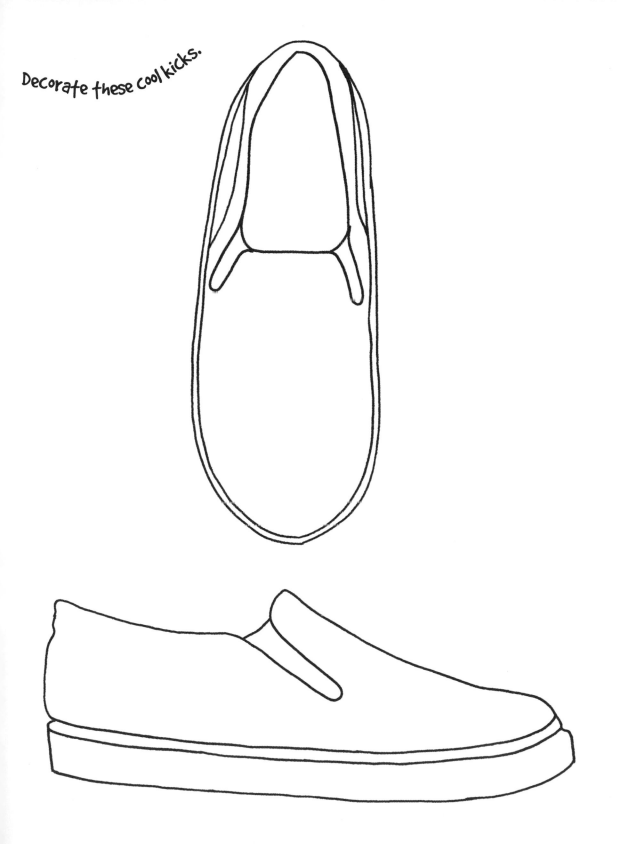

A-ha! What does the astronomer see? Finish drawing the scene.

Decorate this far-out van!

Aren't you crazy for paisley? Continue doodling the pattern.

Butterflies, flutter by . . . now doodle and decorate some of your own.

Add more to the flowers if you wish!

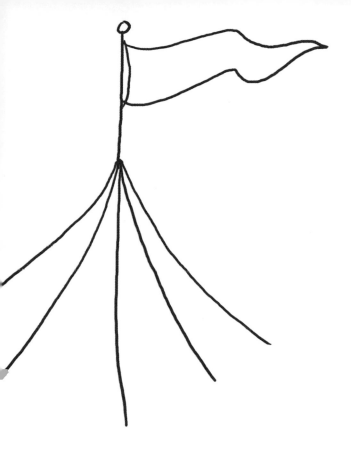

Looks like this fella got some weird
food-on-a-stick at the fair. Draw your own
fair food in the space provided.

Someone's having a birthday party!
Provide party decorations, dessert, and presents.

Design this disco dude's slick threads. Add more dancers if you'd like!

We have a pile o' pumpkins. Carve them into jack-o-lanterns!

What's this dog daydreaming about?

Help this kid finish the big ol' snowman.

Portrait time! What do you look like now?
Include props and surroundings.

You just moved in!
Draw the layout for your awesome
new living room.

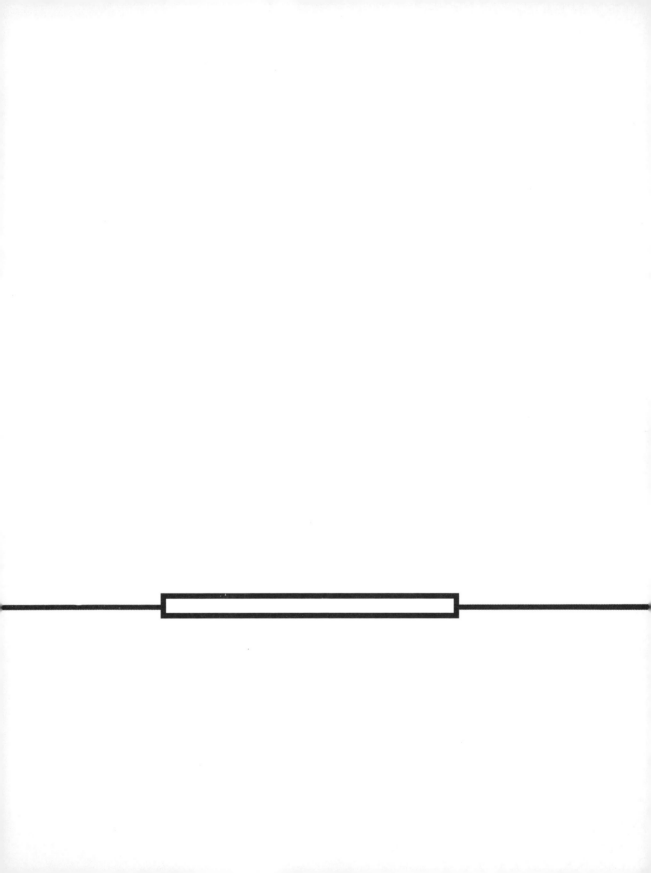

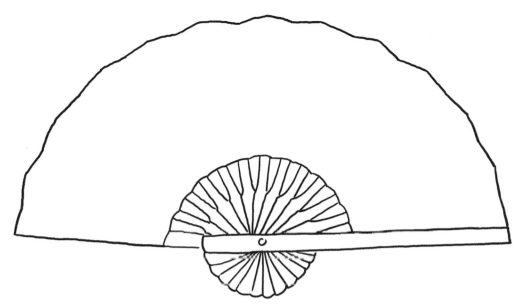

Add some fancy details to these fantastic fans.

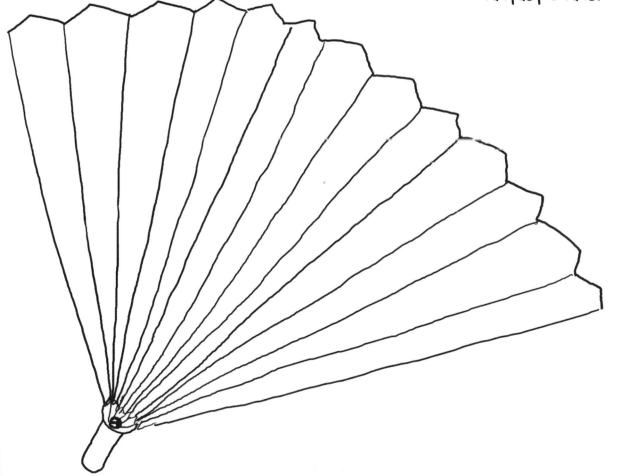

These dog-walkers certainly have their hands full!

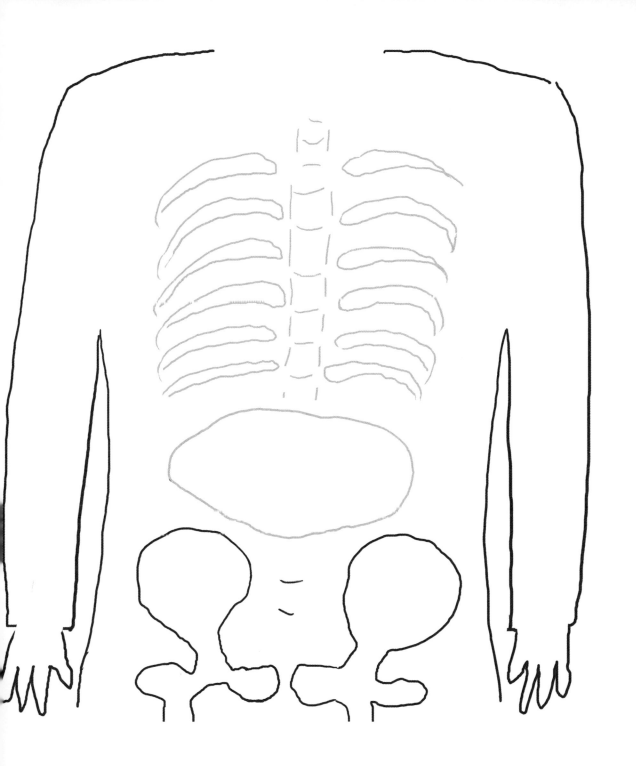

Uh-oh! What did this person swallow?

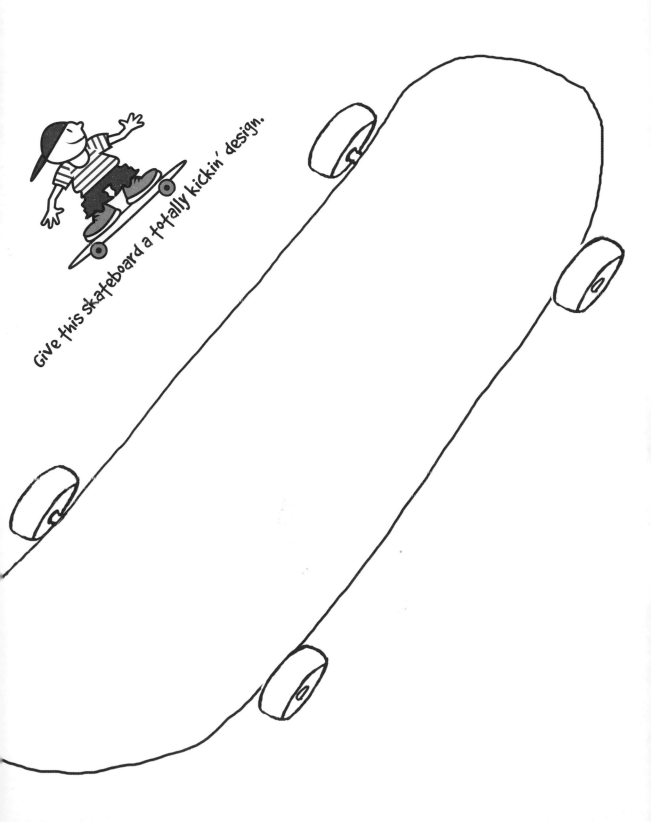

Give this skateboard a totally kickin' design.

You see what we were going for.
Now it's your turn to draw the repeating pattern!

Give this gal some
new ink.

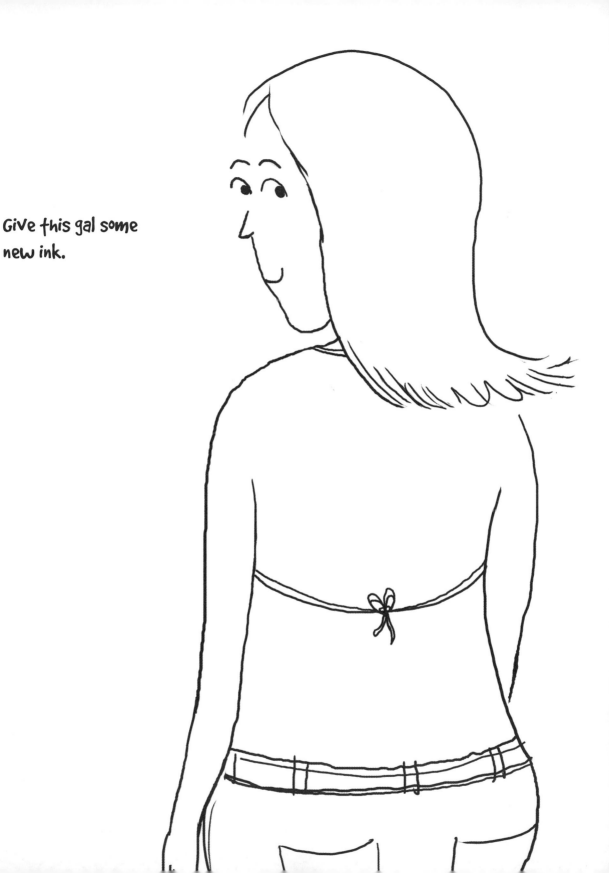

Finish the rest of this dry desert scene.

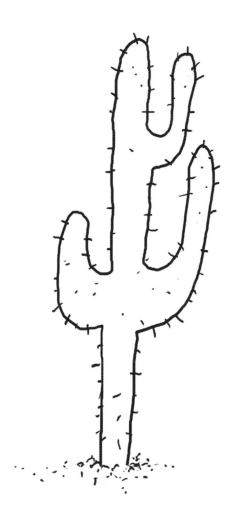

Looks like you had a great vacation! Finish the photos of the places you visited.

Add hair, features, and whatever else you'd like
to these lovely lady mannequins.

Use your noggin to develop your very own pattern out of these squares.

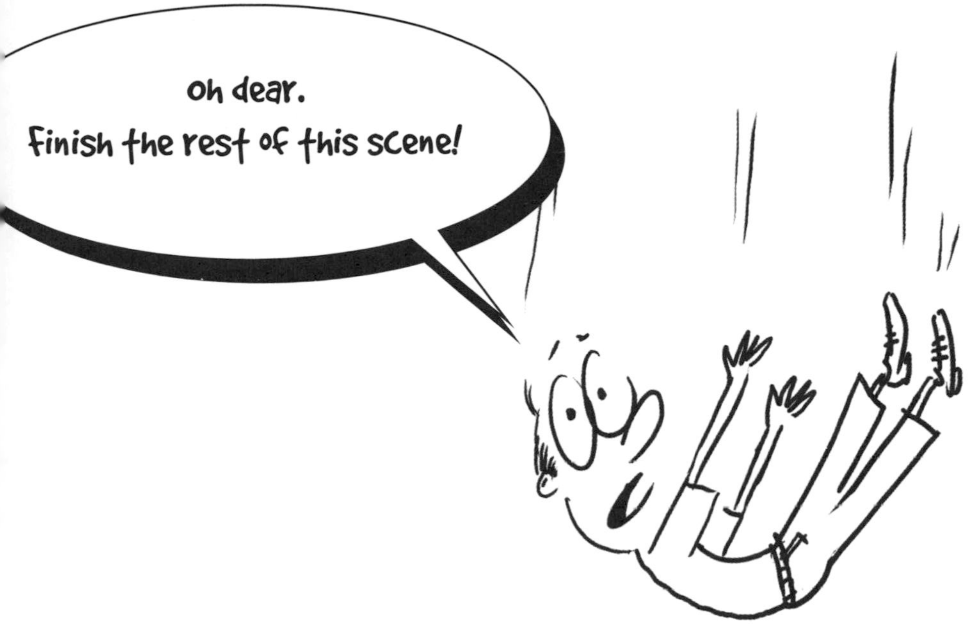
oh dear.
Finish the rest of this scene!

Draw the remaining carousel animals.
Don't be afraid to go wild with it!

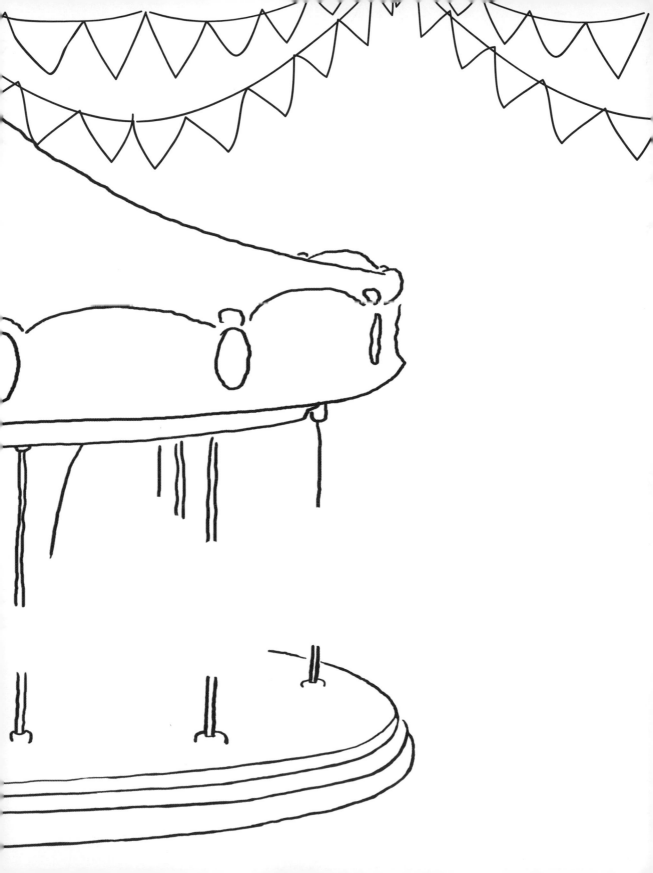

Add more fruit to the bowl.

apple stem stem

Banana Banana

Bowl Bowl Bowl Bowl Bowl Bowl Bowl Bowl Bowl Bowl
Bowl Bowl Bowl Bowl Bowl Bowl Bowl Bowl Bowl Bowl
Bowl Bowl Bowl Bowl Bowl Bowl Bowl Bowl Bowl
Bowl Bowl Bowl Bowl Bowl Bowl Bowl Bowl Bowl
Bowl Bowl Bowl Bowl Bowl Bowl Bowl Bowl
Bowl Bowl Bowl Bowl Bowl Bowl Bowl
Bowl Bowl Bowl Bowl Bowl Bowl
Bowl Bowl Bowl Bowl Bowl
Bowl Bowl Bowl Bowl
Bowl Bowl

Greetings! Finish the rest of this extraterrestrial scene.

We started drawing this crazy doodle—keep it going!

Continuing this series of numbers is as easy as 1, 2, 3!

1

outta sight! finish this groovy go-go dancing scene!

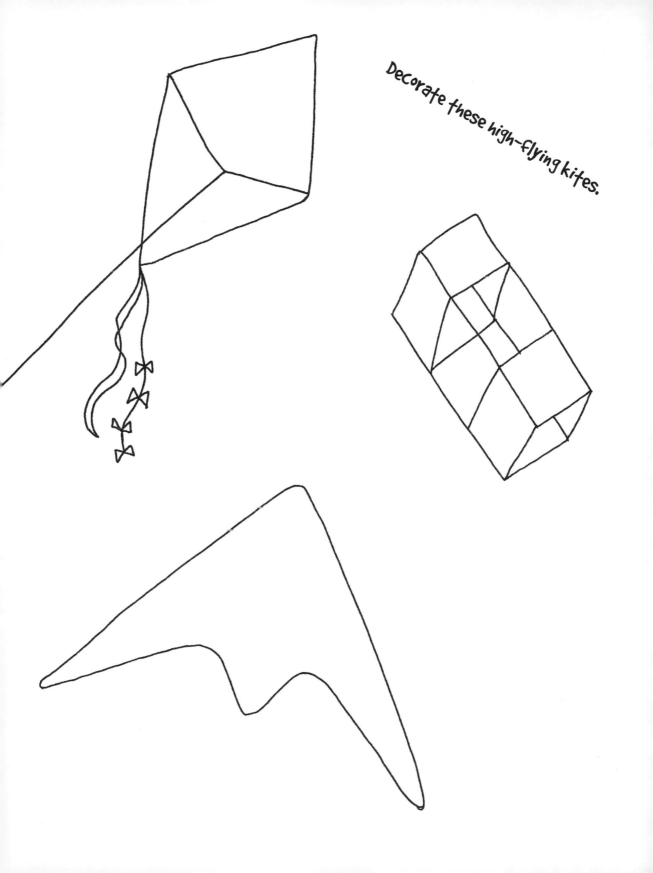

Decorate these high-flying kites.

What is each person riding?

Jazz up these holiday tree ornaments.

Don't get fenced in — color in some of the design to create new patterns!

We've provided plenty of flags and pennants for you to decorate, so get to it!

Something fishy is going on! Add some details to this underwater scene.

Mum's the word! Now keep doodling this showy flower pattern.

Here comes the bride, all dressed in white... Now finish drawing her beautiful wedding dress and add details to the festive occasion!

Pimp this motorcycle, and draw the biker who will be riding it!

color in the pattern to make new designs.

This haughty woman is wearing a large, ornate headpiece called a fascinator. Make hers bigger and even more ridiculous! Use the free space to draw others.

Fill the canvases in the museum.
Now *that's* what we call art!

Fill this junk drawer with odds and ends!

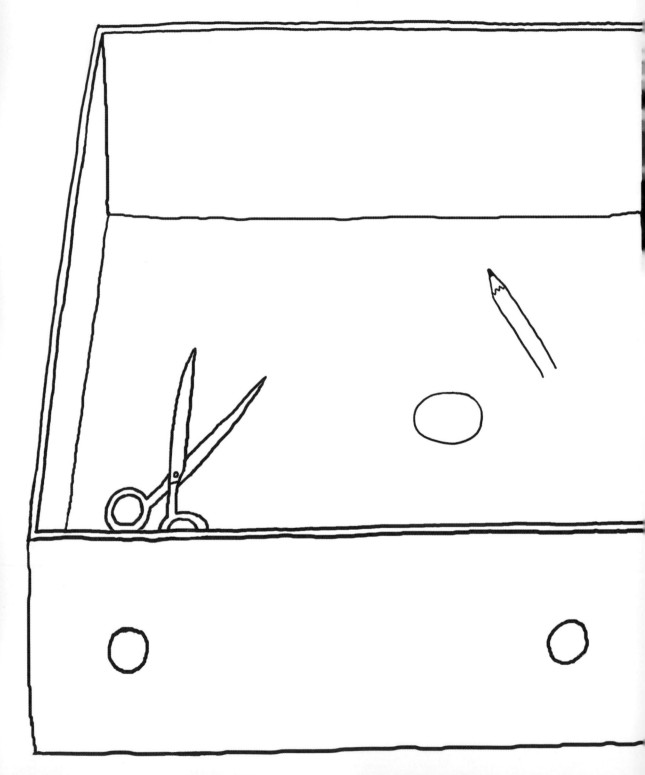

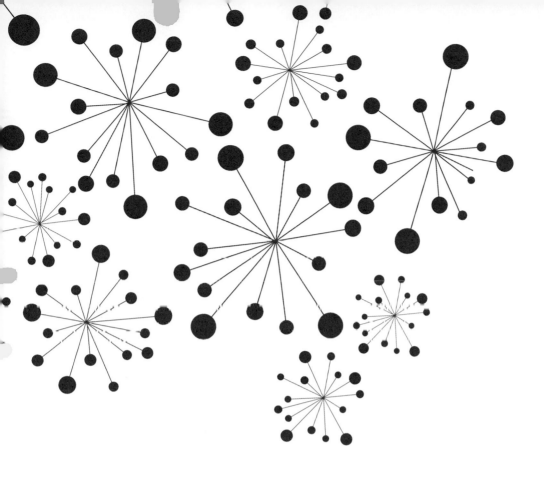

keep doodling these spangles.

Public transportation ain't no picnic. Draw what's going on inside the bus.

Don't tap on the glass — just draw what's inside the fish tank.

Looks like someone got ahold of a crayon! Draw what happens next in the last panel.

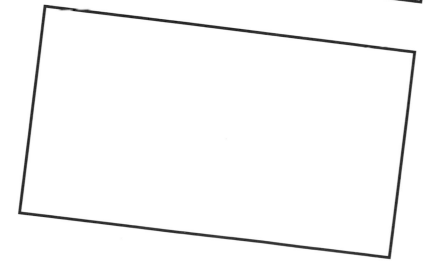

It's time for a Hawaiian luau! Finish drawing this party scene.

TGIF! Finish drawing this office scene.

Dum-dum-de-dum! Doodle some dancers
at this wedding reception.

Add more tasty treats! (Try not to drool.)

It's family portrait time!
Be sure to include props and surroundings.

You just moved into your new house!
Draw the layout for your bedroom.

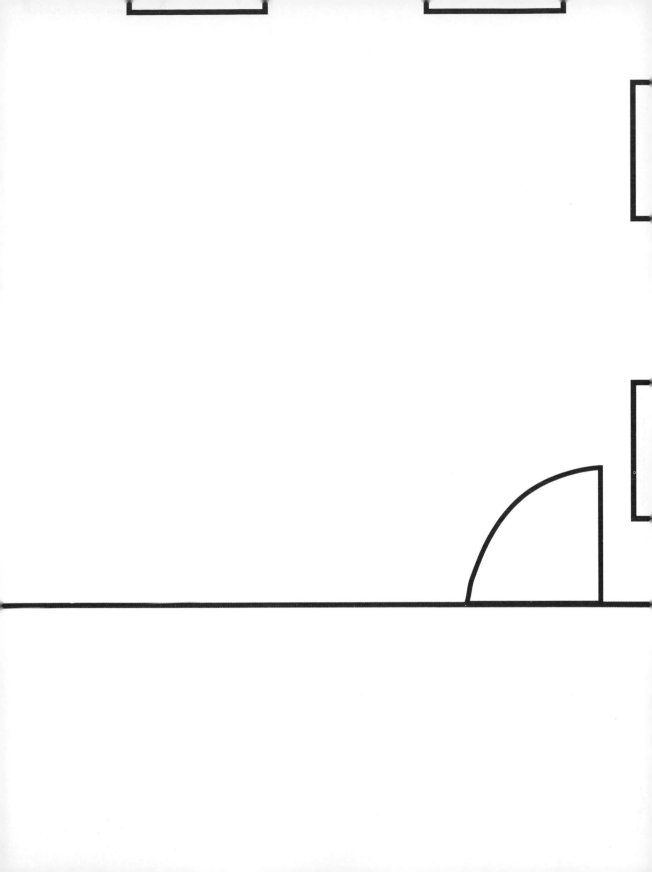

Color in the pattern to make new designs.

You've just published a sci-fi novel! Draw the rest of the cover illustration, and don't forget to give it an out-of-this-world title.

finish drawing the alphabet!

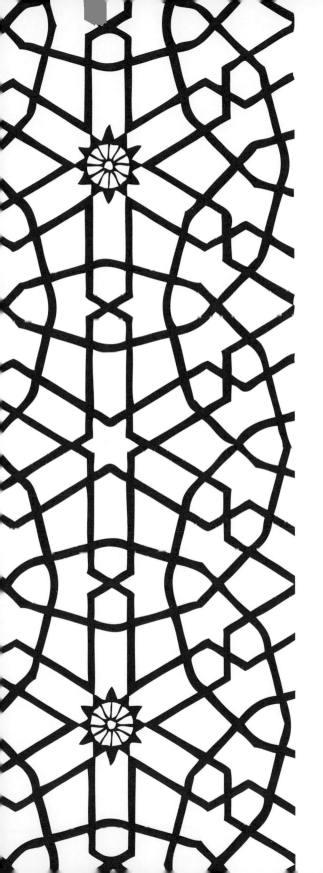

Draw the mirror image of this pattern.

Portrait time! What will you look like in ten years?
Include props and surroundings.

Drum solo! Decorate this rocker's kit.

Rugged, debonair, or just plain weird? Add features to these male mannequins.

I'M WITH STUPID

You have a lot of T-shirts to design. Get to work!

What prizes will the kid win if he knocks over the cans?

Your cupboards are bare! Keep tossing items in the grocery cart to restock your kitchen.

Zowie! What villain is our hero fighting?

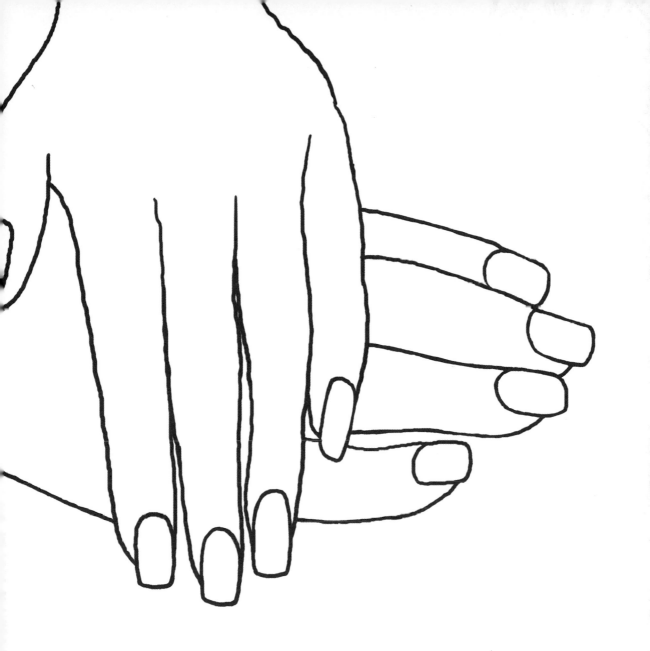

Someone just got a mani! Decorate these freshly polished nails.

Draw the rest of this thrilling battle scene!

Is it a pile of work, or is it a pile of cash? Draw what's inside the briefcase.

Hey, don't act like you're too cool for school. Keep doodling this star-spangled patt
but don't rule out coming up with something of your own.